JUL 1 2 2013

Wild BIKING

Off-Road Mountain Biking

NEIL CHAMPION

A⁺

Smart Apple Media

Published by Smart Apple Media, an imprint of Black Rabbit Books
P.O. Box 3263, Mankato, Minnesota 56002
www.blackrabbitbooks.com

Printed in the United States of America at Corporate Graphics,
North Mankato, Minnesota

Library of Congress Cataloging-in-Publication Data
Champion, Neil.
 Wild biking : off-road mountain biking / by Neil Champion.
     p. cm. -- (Adventure outdoors)
 Includes bibliographical references and index.
 Summary: "Introduces readers to the sport of mountain biking by
teaching how to size up your own bike, the gear needed to ride
and repair your bike, and techniques and tricks of mountain biking.
Includes famous mountain bike trails around the world, labeled
diagrams, and reading quiz"--Provided by publisher.
 ISBN 978-1-59920-811-4 (library binding : alk. paper)
 1. Mountain biking--Juvenile literature. I. Title.
 GV1506.C43 2013
 796.63--dc23
                            2012004781

Created by Appleseed Editions Ltd,
Designed and illustrated by Guy Callaby
Edited by Mary-Jane Wilkins
Picture research by Su Alexander

PO1443
2-2012

9 8 7 6 5 4 3 2 1

Contents

Let's Go Biking!

Mountain biking is one of the most popular adventure sports of all time. It is also one of the most modern, as it dates back to only the late 1970s.

In 1979, Americans Gary Fisher and Charlie Kelly set up a business that made bikes that people could ride off-road. Since then, people all over the world have bought tough bikes that will take them over forest tracks and mountain trails, along river banks, and even through deserts. The mountain bike revolution has touched the lives of millions of people wherever they live.

Above *Bike shops all around the world sell mountain bikes.*

Amazing FACTS

There are many types of mountain biking: cross-country, free riding, endurance racing, downhill, and extreme events. The highest race in the world is held in Tibet, with a view of Mount Everest. Competitors ride as high as 18,050 ft. (5,500 m), where the air is so thin it leaves them gasping. The longest ever mountain bike race ran for 2,700 mi. (4,345 km) from Canada to Mexico through the Rocky Mountains.

Taking Up the Challenge

Few things are as exciting as riding a bike down steep bumpy tracks through woods, over riverbeds, and deep into the hills. Riders need good bike-handling skills, strength, and courage to take on the challenge. Are you ready to feel the thrill of the ride?

Mountain biking is a sport that can appeal to the whole family.

TRUE Survivors

One Sunday in the summer of 1998, 17-year-old Kevin Anderson was dropped off at the start of the Slickrock Bike Trail in Utah. He told his parents that he'd ride around the short practice trail and meet them an hour later. When he didn't turn up, his parents eventually called the emergency services. Several hours later, a search and rescue team found Kevin. He had decided to ride off the small **circuit** and go for a much longer and more challenging ride, despite having no map, lights, spare clothing, or food and water. He became lost and was overtaken by darkness. He was rescued unharmed but was cold, thirsty, and hungry.

What Is Mountain Biking?

Mountain biking involves riding off-road over rough ground, which is often steep and can be dangerous. The bikes that have been developed since the 1970s to deal with this tough **terrain** have special **frames**, brakes, gears, tires, and **suspension**.

TRUE Survivors

Kenny Belaey is a 28-year-old Belgian mountain biker who has won many competitions and undertaken some amazing stunts. In 2011, he traveled to Cape Town, South Africa, and carried his 20-pound (9 kg) bike to the top of Table Mountain while it was still dark (it is too steep to ride up). He was at the top by sunrise and then performed some amazing stunts at 3,280 feet (1,000 m), including **wheelies** on the edge of cliffs and jumping 10-foot (3 m) gaps (called gapping) over sheer drops. To top it off, he hopped up onto the cable car wires high above the ground and rode over them. A mistake at any time would have meant a fall to his death.

The Bike

Today's bikes are designed to cope with the various styles of riding, including downhill, cross-country, dirt jumping, and trial biking. But there are also general mountain bikes that can handle most terrain. They all have strong frames that can withstand bumps and falls, thick tires to grip dirt, soil, mud, or sand, and gears to help riders go uphill on unstable ground. Some also have suspension on the front or rear to help cushion the rider from big jolts and to **absorb** the **impact** of riding over rough ground.

Amazing FACTS

The Cliffs of Moher in County Clare on the west coast of Ireland are more than 650 feet (200 m) high and are a top tourist attraction. About a million people come to walk the 5-mile (8 km) path that runs between the cliff walls and the sea each year. In 2010, intrepid mountain bikers Hans Rey and Steve Peat cycled the trail. As they recalled, the trail included a ledge just 4 inches (10 cm) wide, and they jumped gaps with hundreds of feet of empty space to fall into if they got it wrong!

Mountain Bike Trails

There are mountain bike trails in most countries all over the world. They range from paved trails in towns and cities suitable for the whole family to dangerous mountain descents for experts only. Some have been specially made and others are adapted from ski slopes, dirt tracks, or mountain paths.

World's Best Mountain Bike Trails

1. Whistler, British Colombia, Canada has a 3,940-foot (1,200 m) descent with lots of jumps on the way down. A lift helps riders back up.

2. Les Gets, French Alps has two downhill courses and more than 120 miles (200 km) of biking trails.

3. Cwmcarn, South Wales has the Twrch Trail, a 9-mile (15 km) long purpose-built mountain bike trail, that suits all abilities.

4. Cancha Carrera, Chile is one of the best high mountain bike trails in the world—but only for experienced bikers.

5. Dirt Park, South Island, New Zealand is an advanced 1.2-mile (2 km) downhill thrill ride.

6. Mount Buller, Australia is a ski resort in winter and taken over by mountain bikes the rest of the year. There are four exciting trails to choose from.

7. Moab, Utah is one of the best places for mountain biking and is suitable for all abilities. The Slickrock bike trail is more than 9 miles (15 km) long and one of the best for advanced riders.

The Yungas Road near La Paz in Bolivia, the most dangerous road in the world

TRUE Survivors

When Michael Liebreich and Katherine Henderson read about the most dangerous road in the world, they wanted to try it. The Yungas Road (also known as Death Road) is in Bolivia and runs 43 miles (69 km) from the capital city, La Paz, to Coroico. A vehicle goes over the edge once every two weeks and about 200 people are killed here every year. Landslides and rockfalls are regular occurrences, and the road is constantly under repair.

None of this stops mountain bikers from attempting to ride along it and experiencing its amazing 40-mile (64 km) descent. Liebreich and Henderson set off in May 2004, only to become involved in trying to save a French cyclist who had fallen over the edge in a moment's loss of concentration, landing 164 feet (50 m) below. These cyclists learned that you need superior biking skills to travel the Yungas Road and arrive in one piece.

Getting Started

Mountain biking is good for fitness, offers plenty of thrills, and is fantastic fun. To take part, you need a bike you understand and can adapt to suit your size and style of riding.

Joining a Club

Finding a club is one of the best ways to start, and it will help you meet other cyclists your age. You might be able to rent a bike and try out the sport before you decide to buy one. Clubs offer expert help from experienced adults, as well as hints and tips from other bikers. You will have an opportunity to learn and develop your skills in a safe environment. Find out whether your school has a mountain bike club. If it doesn't, why not set one up?

Information Sources

Many organizations have scouts and guides who offer training in mountain biking. Most countries have national cycling organizations, too, offering information and advice on buying your first mountain bike and learning the basic skills. Your local bike shop may have staff who can answer questions and give you hints on how to get started.

Amazing FACTS

Once you've mastered the basics of mountain biking, the sky is the limit. This was true for the young Spanish mountain biker, Bienve Aguado. In January 2011, he made the first ever double front flip on a mountain bike in Barcelona, Spain. He was towed by motorcycle toward a dirt ramp more than 23 feet (7 m) high, raced up the ramp, and took off at the top. He flipped over twice in midair and landed on the down-slope on the other side of the dirt ramp.

TRUE Survivors

Competitors taking part in extreme mountain biking are always at risk for injuries. Downhill bikers wear body armor, a neck brace, and a full-face helmet to protect themselves from injury when they fall. Even with all this gear, 17-year-old downhill mountain biker Manon Carpenter broke her arm in 2010, the weekend before the World Junior Championship downhill race. She had a metal plate implanted in her arm and was back to her training. In September 2011, she claimed the title of World Junior Champion at the competition in Switzerland.

What Is a Mountain Bike?

A modern mountain bike is designed to ride over a wide variety of surfaces—including rocks, mud, dirt, and sand—as well as to go steeply uphill and downhill. It is strong, with powerful brakes, lots of gears, tough knobby tires, and even front and rear shock absorbers.

seat

handlebars

seat post

head tube

top tube

rear brake

front brake

derailleur gear

down tube

spokes

knobby tire

chain

Made for Mountains

Knobby tires grip uneven and shifting ground much better than ordinary, flat road tires. Some mountain bikers let some air out of their tires to give them greater stability. This means that on a road, mountain bikes (MTBs for short) are slow—there is lots of **friction** in big tires. Disc brakes grip the center of the wheel rather than the rim as on ordinary brakes, which means that they do not get so clogged with dirt. MTBs have between 21 and 27 gears, which allow you to cycle over steep muddy hills. Shock absorbers in the front forks provide stability and also protect your wrists and elbows from the jolting of riding on a hard rocky surface.

Amazing FACTS

The longest mountain bike trail in the world is the Great Divide Trail. It runs from Banff in Canada south through the Rocky Mountains all the way to the Mexican border. It is more than 2,485 miles (4,000 km) long and a fit cyclist takes about 70 days to travel its length, riding 25 to 62 miles (40 to 100 km) a day.

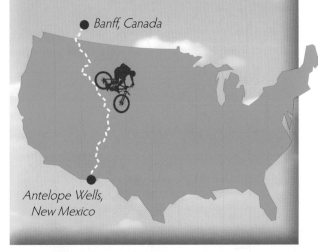

Banff, Canada

Antelope Wells, New Mexico

WORLD'S STRONGEST BIKE

An American company called Delta & Sports has made an incredibly strong and also see-through bike. The frame is made from carbon fibers mixed with **Kevlar** fibers (very strong synthetic fibers), woven into a tube to make the bike frame. It looks strange but is stronger than steel or **titanium**. A bike made from this wonder material costs around $10,000!

The Right Gear

Mountain biking gear should be practical and light to keep you warm in cold weather and cool and dry when it is hot. You should expect to take some falls—they're all part of the fun, but people can be injured.

Clothing

You can wear ordinary clothing: T-shirts, sweatshirts, shorts or pants, and tennis shoes. If you are riding in sunshine, wear a hat. If the weather is cold and wet, make sure you have a waterproof jacket and fleece. Padded shorts or pants make longer and harder rides more comfortable.

helmet

windproof jacket

A mountain biker geared up and ready to ride

biking shoes

Above *A full helmet protects your face if you fall.*

Body Protection

Helmet All MTB riders wear helmets: they save lives and protect against head injuries and **concussions**. Two thirds of people killed in biking accidents die because of head injuries. Always wear a helmet—on-road or off-road. Modern helmets are light and allow air to reach your head. Downhill racers wear helmets with face guards.

Gloves When you fall, your hands are the first to hit the ground. Gloves prevent cuts and bruises and help absorb the shock of an impact.

Shockproof glasses These protect your eyes from mud and grit thrown up from the trail.

Knee and elbow protectors On tougher trails, these are essential, as knees and elbows usually hit the ground right after your hands when you fall.

Emergency Equipment
If you go on a long trail, take plenty of liquid and food. You can carry it in a **pannier** or on your back in a small backpack. Also consider taking a cell phone, bike lights (in case you return after dark), spare clothing, sunscreen and a sunhat, and possibly even a lightweight shelter in case of emergency.

TRUE Survivors

Caernarfon

Cardiff

Forty-one-year-old Welshman Dave Buchanan is a true survivor. In 2011, he set a record for the longest distance traveled by mountain bike in 48 hours with an epic ride across Wales. The ride took him from Cardiff in the south to Caernarfon in the north and back again; 448 miles (721 km) in all. Most of the ride was off-road, and all the ascents put together would add up to 2.5 times the height of Everest. Altogether, Dave endured 59 hours of nonstop pedaling in rain and a strong wind—an amazing example of mountain biking grit, determination, and survival.

Sizing Your Bike

Your bike needs to be the right size for you to handle. If it is too big or too small, it will feel awkward and out of balance. An experienced person will help you adjust the handlebars and seat so they fit you correctly.

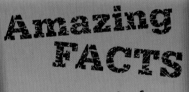

Amazing FACTS

When your bike fits you well and you have had plenty of time to practice your skills, there is no telling what you might achieve. It is important to understand how to handle the bike and where its balance points are. In October 2007, 19-year-old Mads Rasmussen from Denmark performed what must be the world's longest wheelie— riding his mountain bike continuously on just one wheel for an amazing 1.4 miles (2.3 km). As he said, "The trick is the rider's skill and balance ability."

Make sure your bike is the right size for you.

When cycling fast, your leg should be almost straight on the downstroke.

Seat Height

When you sit on your bike with one leg extended, that leg should be almost straight when your foot touches the pedal at the bottom of the downstroke. This is the position which will give you maximum power when riding. If your knees are too high or you can barely reach the pedals, your balance will be affected and your power reduced.

Frame Size

Frames range from 14 inches (35 cm) to 22 inches (56 cm)—extra large. Make sure you have the right size: you shouldn't lean too far over the handlebars or be cramped because the frame is too small. The length of the tube that runs from the handlebars to the seat is important: you need to comfortably reach the handlebars with your elbows slightly bent.

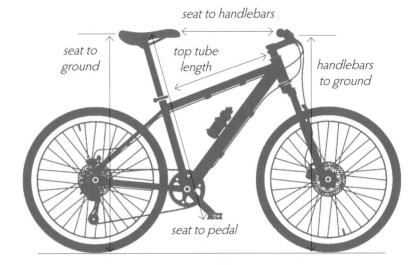

Bike frames come in different sizes. Some parts can be adjusted but others cannot.

TRUE Survivors

American Missy "The Missile" Giove was one of the early champions of downhill mountain bike racing. In her first four years of professional downhill racing, she broke her hand, smashed her kneecap and her heel, broke her wrist, pelvis, collar bone, and her teeth! As one headline put it, "She bicycles down mountains at speeds of up to 56 mph (90 km/h). If she doesn't crash, she wins!"

Bike Repairs

Keep your bike clean and **service** it regularly. Learn how to do simple repairs: they can make the difference between a long push home or continuing your ride. Be prepared, learn the skills, and buy the repair kit before you need it.

What to Carry

If you are going on a long ride, make sure you carry the following:

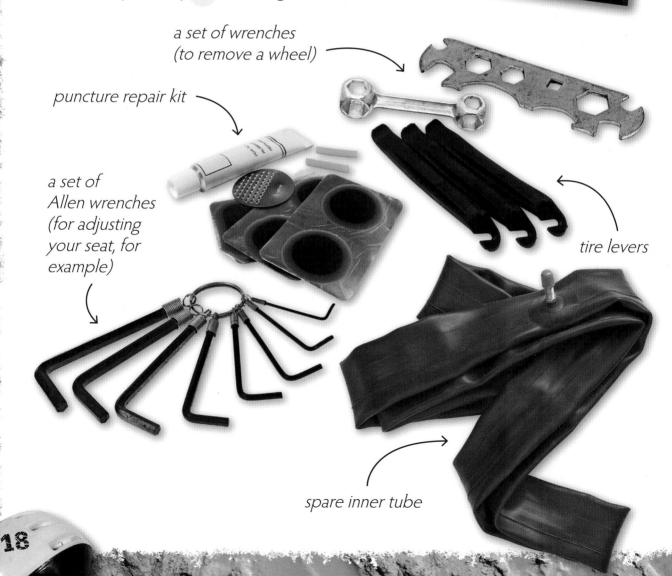

a set of wrenches (to remove a wheel)

puncture repair kit

a set of Allen wrenches (for adjusting your seat, for example)

tire levers

spare inner tube

Mending a Puncture

Keep your tires inflated to the right pressure, check them often for stones and glass, and replace them when they look old and worn. This will reduce the number of punctures you get. This is how you mend a puncture:

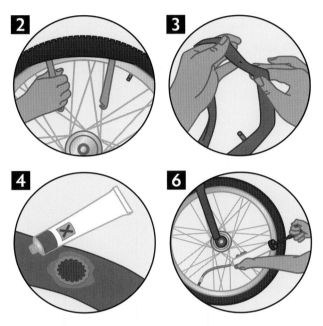

1 Remove the wheel.

2 Remove the tire using tire levers.

3 Find the puncture in your inner tube.

4 Either use a puncture repair kit to put a rubber patch over the puncture or replace the inner tube with a new one.

5 Put the inner tube and tire back on the wheel and put the wheel back on the bike.

6 Pump up the tire and set off again.

If you are out on a ride when you get a puncture, you may be able to pump up the punctured tire and cycle quickly to a place where you can make the repairs —off the road and against a fence or on some flat ground off a steep trail.

Gears and Brakes

Learn how to make adjustments to your gears and brakes. Many clubs run bicycle repair workshops where you can learn the basic repair and maintenance skills you will need.

TRUE Survivors

In April 2010, 30-year-old Kevin Myatt was enjoying a day out on a bike trail in the Whakarewarewa Forest in New Zealand. He gathered speed to take some jumps but lost control and shot over the handlebars, landing on his back. In the crash, the brake lever broke off and got stuck in his hand. He was taken to Rotorua hospital where the lever was successfully removed and he has since made a full recovery.

Basic skills

Once your bike is adjusted to suit your size, the challenge is to learn the handling and the basic skills you need to ride it off-road. Always start on easy terrain and build up your skills to match the difficulty of the trail. Don't bite off more than you can chew!

Look Well Ahead

Learn to scan the path in front of you for dangers and **hazards**. The faster you go, the farther ahead you need to look. Check the trail for deep puddles, potholes, large mud patches, and obstacles such as rocks, tree branches—even other cyclists. If you take action early enough to avoid them, you shouldn't need to brake quickly, which can lead to a skid and a fall. Try to steer as smoothly as possible.

Braking

Beginners often brake too sharply, which can lead to problems—you may even fly over the handlebars! Cover your brakes with your hands at all times, anticipate problems, and slow down in good time. Learn which is your front brake and which is the back. When braking to take a corner, make sure that you have stopped braking by the time you go around the bend.

Pedal Power

For powerful pedaling, try to continue the motion on the upstroke as well as on the downstroke. That way you get more out of your effort than just pushing down and then relaxing. Think of the pedaling action as an almost complete circle of effort.

A mountain biker lands on his hands and knees after falling on a steep descent.

Using Gears

Again try to look ahead and decide which gear you need to be in and change well in advance. When you see a hill coming up, change down through the gears while still on flat ground. This way you won't have to grind the gears while struggling uphill.

Advanced Cycling

Once you have mastered the basics, you may be ready to take on some tougher terrain. Take advice from an experienced adult and aim to progress steadily without attempting too much too soon.

Below are some techniques you need to learn to deal with steeper, longer, and scarier trails. Remember to wear protective clothing while doing these.

Find Your Balance Point

Being able to brake slowly or use a hill to bring you to a stop without putting your feet on the ground takes practice. Aim to balance your bike and yourself without falling to one side or the other. Start by facing up a gentle slope. Push forward while standing on the pedals and twist your handlebars to one side. See how long you can stay there. Try again and see whether you can do it for longer. This technique will give you confidence to stop on a track while still riding your bike. You need to master it before learning other techniques, such as hopping.

TRUE Survivors

In September 2007, Austrian racing cyclist Markus Stökl set a world record for being the fastest person on a mountain bike. He traveled to La Parva in Chile and bombed down a 1-mile (1.6 km) long track that was on a 45 degree slope. His maximum speed was 130 mph (210 km/h). At that speed, one small mistake could lead to a crash that might prove fatal.

A group of riders out for an adventure on a mountain bike trail

Steep Downhill

Going steeply downhill takes skill and can be scary. You need to use your brakes at all times and control your balance. Standing up helps, shifting your weight forward and backward to cope with the terrain. Try to keep your weight on your feet—not your arms—and stay relaxed. This helps you respond to the shape of the trail and its many bumps.

First Small Drop

Going over your first small step is a big moment. Try to stay relaxed as you approach. Have a plan. Will you go over one wheel at a time, landing on your front wheel? If the drop is steep on the other side, you might need to land with both tires on the ground at the same time. If it is a bigger drop, you may even have to land rear tire first.

This advanced rider is well protected for a steep descent on rough terrain.

Tricks and Stunts

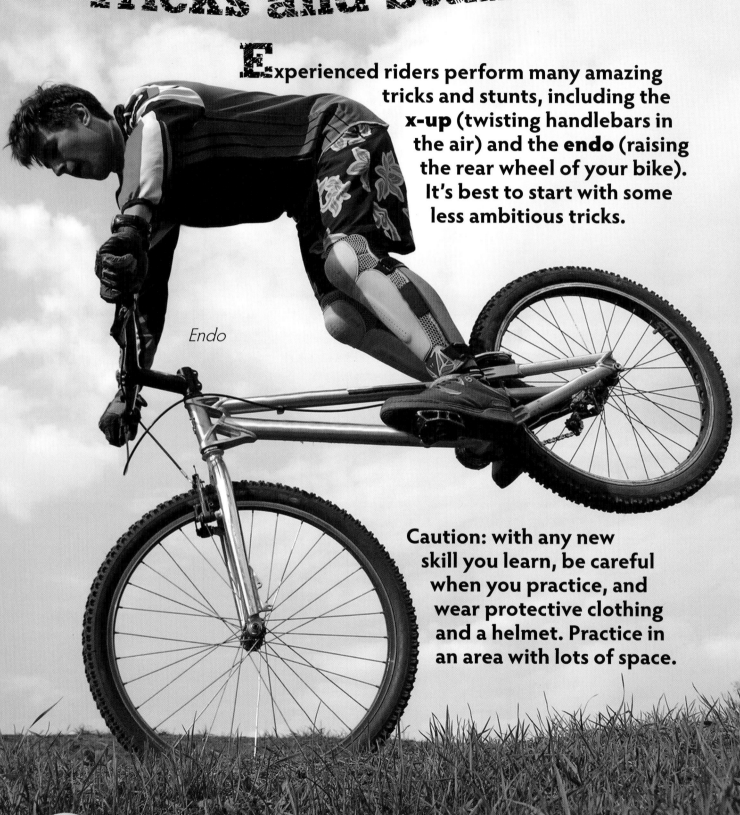

Experienced riders perform many amazing tricks and stunts, including the **x-up** (twisting handlebars in the air) and the **endo** (raising the rear wheel of your bike). It's best to start with some less ambitious tricks.

Endo

Caution: with any new skill you learn, be careful when you practice, and wear protective clothing and a helmet. Practice in an area with lots of space.

Front Wheel Lift

Cycle along slowly, and lift the front wheel a little off the ground by tightening your arms and pulling back on the handlebars. Shift your weight toward the back of the bike too. Don't be too ambitious or you might flip backward! Once you have mastered this, you could progress to doing a wheelie.

Rear Wheel Lift

Ride along and then apply your brakes. At the same time, push down into the pedals and shift your weight forward over the handlebars. Try to lift your rear wheel a couple of inches off the ground. Once you become more confident, you will be able to lift it higher.

Bunny hop

Amazing FACTS

The world record for a single standing bunny hop is held by Spain's Benito Ros Charral. In 2009 in Heubach, Germany, he hopped over a pole set an incredible 4.66 feet (1.42 m) high from a standing start.

Riding steps

Bunny Hops

Put an obstacle in front of your bike, such as a piece of wood, to hop your bike over. Start by lifting the front wheel over the piece of wood. Next, try lifting your rear wheel over the wood. Then try lifting both wheels off together—this is the **bunny hop**.

Riding Steps

Start with just a couple of steps and build up. Cycle slowly to the top of the steps and let your front wheel go over. Stand on the pedals, keep relaxed and springy, and let your weight go backward. This will help you control the second step. Once you are comfortable with two steps, try tackling a few more.

Mountain Bike Racing

Today there are mountain biking world championships and a world cup series. It first became an Olympic sport at the 1996 Olympics, when downhill races were held.

There are many exciting race competitions you can follow or even take part in. Here are some of them:

Downhill racers set off at different times on a steep downhill track. The winner is the fastest person to get down the track successfully. There are many thrills and spills on the way!

Free ride compares the skills and techniques of riders. Four riders set off

Mountain bike racing is the ultimate challenge for this young competitor.

over a course on which they have to do tricks and race for the finish line.

Dirt jumping also tests the skills of the riders, who have to make lots of jumps from hills of dirt high in the air, performing tricks along the way.

Competition FACTS

The youngest person to win a mountain bike world championship title was just 16. In 2001, Sam Hill from Australia came in third in the championships at Vail in Colorado.

The 2011 world downhill champion is Danny Hart from Great Britain. He sealed his success at Champery in France. Competing in pouring rain, he beat the rest of the field in an extraordinary run down a steep wooded trail to win the title.

Cross-country takes place on a trail about 5 miles (8 km) long over varied ground. All the racers start together and compete against each other to finish first.

Marathon racing takes place over long distances. Racers compete on a trail about 50 miles (80 km) long in mountainous terrain.

Cross-country mountain bike racing in winter conditions presents huge challenges.

What do you know about mountain biking?

Are you ready to take on the challenge of a steep mountain trail? Could you take a drop over a 3-foot (1 m) rock, stop and balance on your bike, or anticipate danger along a trail? Take this quiz to find out just how much you know about the thrill ride known as mountain biking. The answers are on page 31.

1 **Which statement is correct?**
a The longest mountain bike race runs from Canada to Mexico through the Rocky Mountains.
b The highest mountain bike races take place on Everest.
c Mountain biking started in the 1970s in California.
d You cannot start mountain biking until you are 18 years old.

2 **Mountain biking is the skill of pushing your bike up mountains.**
True or false?

3 **The Cliffs of Moher on the west coast of Ireland are home to one of the scariest mountain bike trails on the planet.**
True or false?

4 **Which of these is not a hazard you would expect to find on a mountain bike trail?**
a Tree branches
b Muddy puddles
c Steep terrain
d A shark

5 **Where is the Yungas Road, one of the most dangerous routes to cycle in the world?**
a France   **b** Bolivia   **c** Hawaii   **d** South Africa

6 **An endo is:**
a Stopping suddenly and going up on to your front tire
b The trick of being able to cycle backward
c A stunt in which you take off and land on your back wheel
d A term your friends shout out when you cross the finishing line of a downhill race

7 **The world's strongest bike is made from**
a Wood
b Titanium
c Aluminium
d Kevlar and carbon fibers

8 **You don't need a helmet on a downhill mountain bike trail.**
True or false?

9 **When sitting on your seat, the foot of your straightened leg should touch the pedal on its downstroke in a correctly sized bike.**
True or false?

10 **Which of the following don't you need in your bike repair kit?**
a Tire levers
b Puncture repair kit
c Map of the countryside
d A set of Allen wrenches

11 **Dirt jumping is:**
a What you do when you try to avoid muddy or dirty parts of a mountain bike trail
b A type of mountain bike competition in which the riders have to perform a series of stunts taking off from dirt mounds
c Avoiding bad comments from your friends about your style of riding
d A training exercise to get you fit for mountain biking

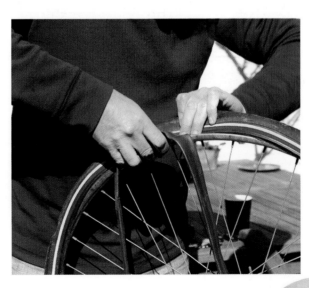

Glossary

absorb To soak up; on a mountain bike, this refers to the cushioning effect a springy bike suspension has when you go over rocky ground.

bunny hop A trick where the rider lifts both wheels off the ground to hop over an obstacle.

circuit A course around a track or trail, usually finishing at the point where you started.

concussion A serious head injury that can damage the brain.

endo An uncontrolled endo is a sudden stop which locks the front wheel, sending the back wheel up in the air and the rider over the handlebars; in a controlled endo, the rider stops and balances on the front wheel.

frame The main structure of a bike made of tubes of metal with the seat and two wheels attached.

friction When two surfaces touch and rub against each other, friction occurs; mountain bike tires have a bigger surface area than other bike tires, creating more friction.

hazards Anything that can cause you harm is a hazard—tree branches, mud patches, holes, steep drops, and so on.

impact Impact is the force that comes up through the bike and into your body from the bumpy ground you are riding on.

Kevlar A very strong man-made material used to make a range of things from bike tires to body armor.

pannier A type of bag that fits on the back of a bike to carry supplies and equipment.

service Checking all the main parts (such as brakes and gears), replacing any worn parts, and oiling the chain and wheel hubs.

suspension Bikes with suspension built into the front forks feel springy; the suspension helps to cushion the bumps coming up from the rough ground through the tires.

terrain The type of landscape and ground that you ride over—for example, a muddy forest trail or a rocky mountain track.

titanium A very strong and light metal that does not rust easily.

wheelie The skill of being able to cycle along on just your back wheel.

x-up A stunt jump done on a mountain bike that involves turning the handlebars 180° into an "x" shape while you fly through the air.

Websites

www.imba.com The International Mountain Bike Association
www.mbr.co.uk The Mountain Bike Rider
www.mountainbike.com Mountain Bike website
www.ambc.com.au Australian Mountain Biking
www.mountainbike.co.nz New Zealand Mountain Biking

Books

Mastering Mountain Bike Skills Brian Lopes and Lee McCormack, Human Kinetics, 2010

Mountain Biking (Get Outdoors) Paul Mason, PowerKids Press, 2011

Mountain Biking: Techniques and Tricks (Rad Sports) Aaron Rosenberg, Rosen Publishing Group, 2003

Mountain Biking (Torque: Action Sports) Jack David, Bellwether Media, 2008

Quiz Answers

1 a, c   **5** b   **9** True

2 False   **6** a   **10** c

3 True   **7** d   **11** b

4 d   **8** False

Index